Stellwagen

Basin

wagen Bank

Southwest
Corner

Ralph Granata

Point Channel

Race Point

Provincetown
Provincetown
Harbor

CAPE

COD

NATIONAL

SEASHORE

CAPE COD

BAY

Wellfleet
Harbor

Eastham

Boston's South Shore

A PHOTOGRAPHIC PORTRAIT

PHOTOGRAPHY BY
Ralph Granata

NARRATIVE BY
Sara Day

TWIN LIGHTS PUBLISHERS · ROCKPORT, MASSACHUSETTS

First published in the United States of America by:

Twin Lights Publishers, Inc.
8 Hale Street
Rockport, Massachusetts 01966
Telephone: (978) 546-7398
http://www.twinlightspub.com

ISBN: 978-1-934907-15-3

10 9 8 7 6 5 4 3 2 1

Dedication

For Cindy, who teaches me each day that to see,
one must look with their heart as well as their
eyes. I love you with both.

Acknowledgements

As I traveled the side roads and main streets
of Boston's South Shore, I came to understand
that working on a book is a personal, yet not a
solitary journey.

To my sister Barbara - thank you for the hours
spent working to obtain photo releases. Your
efforts made my work achievable.

To Hal Goldstein and Eric Frazer who assisted
on several shoots – thank you both for your
friendship and trusted counsel.

Ralph Granata

(*opposite*) Cohasset, Massachusetts

(*frontispiece*) Marshfield, Massachusetts

(*jacket front*) Scituate, Massachusetts

(*jacket back*) Marshfield, Massachusetts

Book design by:
SYP Design & Production, Inc.
www.sypdesign.com

Printed in China

Between Boston and Cape Cod is a certain stretch of coastline that rolls along quaint, small towns, separating them from the deep and moody Atlantic Ocean. From Quincy to Plymouth, the South Shore unfolds along Massachusetts Bay with an unimaginable beauty that has inspired artists and writers since they first stepped off the *Mayflower* in 1620.

Calm creeks meander through salt marshes of green and gold, roaring waves pound jagged granite, and centuries-old barns hold tight to their secrets — it's all part of an incredible orchestra that plays some of New England's greatest melodies. Photographer Ralph Granata has captured the essence of this exquisite place. Through his discerning eye, lifestyles — both past and present — are brought forth in detail, from Adams National Historic Park to Plimoth Plantation.

Boston's South Shore is unpretentious, a mix of suburban towns and industrial small cities that, with all their unique offerings, have somehow managed to avoid the massive throngs of tourists that flock to the North Shore, or further south to Cape Cod. Since the end of World War II, many Irish-American families migrated from Boston to towns throughout the South Shore in search of opportunity or an affordable summer retreat. This heavy Irish-American influence has fondly dubbed the South Shore as the "Irish Riviera." Today, the communities of the South Shore boast the highest percentage of Irish-Americans in the country.

With each colorful image, the pages of this book reveal the true splendor of the region, from the majestic beachfront homes on the Hull peninsula, to the maritime charm of coastal towns like Hingham, Scituate, Marshfield, and Duxbury. Boston's South Shore is, by far, the unsung hero of Massachusetts — the Bay State's hidden treasure.

Lighthouse Army of Two (*opposite*)
A true story happened one evening during the War of 1812 when Simon Bates' daughters, Rebecca and Abigail, were in charge of the Scituate Lighthouse. As a British ship approached, the girls played military calls with fife and drum and successfully tricked the enemy who quickly headed away from the phantom militia.

Granite Railway

Designed by railway innovator, Gridley Bryant, the Granite Railway began operating in 1826, transporting granite needed to build the Bunker Hill Monument in Charlestown. The 3-mile railway featured wagons with wheels measuring 6 feet in diameter. The railway is part of the Blue Hills Reservation.

First Commercial Railway

Considered America's first commercial railway, The Granite Railway is a Civil Engineering Landmark. Although the last quarry closed in 1963, visitors can hike the trail to view old quarry sites. The railway is a National Historic Landmark and is overseen by the Department of Conservation and Recreation.

Adams Academy Building *(above)*

Adams Academy preparatory school for boys was founded in 1872 by President John Adams. Fashioned from Quincy granite, the Adams Academy Building was erected on the site of John Hancock's birthplace. Today, this national historical landmark houses the Quincy Historical Society.

Old House *(opposite, top)*

Part of Adams National Historical Park, the Old House was home to four generations of Adamses. Built in 1731, the mansion houses historic artifacts and period furniture. This historic building, along with the adjacent Stone Library with its collection of over 14,000 books, is known as Peacefield.

Thomas Crane Library *(opposite, bottom)*

This granite masterpiece was built in 1882 by architect Henry Hobson Richardson as a tribute to Thomas Crane, a wealthy stone contractor who began his successful business in the Quincy quarries. The grounds of the library were designed by renowned landscape architect Frederick Law Olmsted.

Historical Park Gardens (*above and left*)

The grounds of the Adams National Historical Park include an historic apple orchard and an 18th-century garden bursting with an array of extraordinary annuals and perennials. Landscaping was originally designed by Frederick Law Olmsted. Peacefield, including both the Old House and the Stone Library, is a National Historic Site.

Creeping Ivy (*opposite*)

Creeping ivy works in harmony with the architecture on the grounds of the Adams National Historic Park. The park is made up of several historic structures on approximately 14 acres of land.

Dorothy Quincy Homestead

Black-eyed Susans cheerfully decorate
the grounds of the childhood home of
Dorothy Quincy Hancock, wife of patriot
John Hancock who was the first signer
of the Declaration of Independence.
Period furnishings and artifacts paint a
picture of the day-to-day lifestyles of early
Massachusetts Colony settlers.

Patriotic Homestead

The Quincy Homestead was home to five generations of Quincys, including President John Quincy Adams and Dr. Oliver Wendell Holmes. Built in 1686, the home, with its distinctive gambrel roof, is a significant historical landmark having served as a meeting place for Revolutionary dignitaries.

United First Parish Church *(above)*

The United First Parish Church is known as the "Church of the Presidents." Inside, a plaque marks a pew where United States President John Quincy Adams sat. Presidents John Adams and John Quincy, along with their wives, Abigail Adams and Louisa Catherine Adams, are buried in a crypt within the church.

John Adams *(opposite)*

Designed by sculptor Lloyd Lillie and dedicated in 2001, this bronze statue of the second U.S. President is located in Quincy's City Hall Square. Nicknamed the "Atlas of Independence," President John Adams co-authored the Declaration of Independence and coincidentally died on July 4th.

Stone Upon Stone *(above)*

Constructed in 1828 of Quincy granite, the United First Parish Church was designed by renowned architect Alexander Parris who also designed Boston's Quincy Market. This Greek Revival-style church became a National Historic Landmark in 1970.

Bell Tower *(opposite)*

The United First Parish Church bell tower has undergone an extensive renovation including a new bronze bell, the refurbishing of the 19th-century clock, and new gold leaf on the dome. Church volunteers conduct tours of the church and Presidents' crypt in cooperation with the Adams National Historical Park.

Hancock Cemetery *(above, left, and opposite)*

The Hancock Cemetery includes many fragile grave markers, some dating as far back as the 1630s. Of the many famous residents buried here are Henry Adams, descendent of John Adams, and Colonel John Quincy for whom the city of Quincy was named. Located across from the United First Parish Church, the cemetery itself is named for Reverend John Hancock, father of American patriot John Hancock.

Historic Masonic Temple *(above)*

Located on Hancock Street in Quincy, this Masonic Temple is home to three Masonic Lodges. The massive three-story, Neoclassical-style building includes a ballroom and oak-paneled library.

Temple Details *(opposite)*

Known for guarding valuable treasures, majestic griffins support massive tripod tables that flank the entrance of Quincy's Masonic Temple. The entranceway architecture includes a barrage of Masonic symbols including the well-known square and compass emblem, the keystone, the equilateral triangle, and the Teutonic Cross.

Outcroppings (above)

Because of its deep color and high-polish potential, granite from Quincy quarries was used in the construction of many important landmarks. After the industry boom, quarry cliffs and massive granite outcroppings, such as this, functioned as recreation areas for mountain climbers in training.

USS Salem (opposite, top)

The hallmark of the United States Shipbuilding Museum, the USS Salem was launched in 1947 and served as a flagship for U.S. fleets in the Mediterranean and in the Atlantic. She was decommissioned in 1959, but has since been restored and recommissioned as a member of the Historic Naval Ships Association.

Big Guns (opposite, bottom)

The big guns of the USS Salem are formidable, yet they've never been fired. Her presence alone was enough to keep peace during the tense era of the Cold War. Today, the massive ship serves as a floating classroom, where visitors can explore naval history and the building of this famous heavy cruiser.

Thayer Academy

Prestigious Thayer Academy in Braintree was founded in 1877 by General Sylvanus Thayer, a Braintree native who was the "father" of the U.S. Military Academy at West Point. Thayer is a college preparatory school that includes eight buildings set on a sprawling 24-acre campus.

Weymouth Town Hall

The cornerstone of this Old State House replica was laid in 1928. The original town hall of Weymouth was built in 1852 and was destroyed by fire in 1914. Birthplace of Abigail Adams, wife of John Adams, Weymouth was incorporated into the Massachusetts Bay Colony in 1635.

Ralph Talbot Amphitheater *(above)*

A memorial honoring Weymouth soldiers who served in all U.S. wars, this open-air auditorium provides an historic outdoor venue for this South Shore town. The amphitheater was named for U.S. Marine Second Lieutenant Ralph Talbot, an aviator who was the recipient of the first Medal of Honor.

The Cross of Gray *(opposite)*

U.S. soldiers who made the ultimate sacrifice are honored with this striking cross made of Barre white granite. The Cross of Gray is part of the Weymouth town common, which was dedicated in April of 1930. The monument was crafted according to the same design as a cross at Arlington National Cemetery.

Jason Holbrook Homestead *(top)*

The Jason Holbrook family were some of Weymouth's earliest settlers. Their circa 1763 home comprises the Weymouth Historical Society. It includes a genealogical library dating back to the 1600s and a museum of period artifacts and antiques from the American Revolution, Civil War, and both world wars.

Abigail Adams Homestead *(bottom)*

Abigail Adams was the wife of John Adams and mother of John Quincy Adams, sixth President of the United States. Her Weymouth birthplace is home to the Abigail Adams Historical Society, an organization formed in 1947 to preserve the home of one of America's most admirable patriots.

King Phillip's War Memorial *(opposite)*

At the corner of Middle and Washington Streets, the site of Weymouth's first town hall, is a plaque marking the spot of the town's "last Indian attack" in 1676. Presented by Colonel Frederick Gilbert Bauer in 1930, this location is also believed to be the exact geographic center of the town of Weymouth.

NEAR THIS SITE TOOK PLACE
ON APRIL 19 · 1676
THE LAST INDIAN ATTACK
ON WEYMOUTH
THIS ATTACK WAS THE
HIGH WATER MARK OF
KING PHILIP'S WAR
BEING THE NEAREST POINT TO
BOSTON EVER REACHED BY
KING · PHILIP'S FORCES
——
ERECTED BY THE
SOCIETY OF COLONIAL WARS
IN THE
COMMONWEALTH OF MASSACHUSETTS
ON THE 254TH ANNIVERSARY
OF THE BATTLE

1930

Loring Hall *(above)*

Loring Hall was the brainchild of a group of Hingham women who felt the need for a proper public meeting place in their town. With the help of Colonel Benjamin Loring, their wishes were realized and the building was dedicated in 1852. In 1936, the hall was transformed into a modern movie theater that still retains its original colonial charm.

General Benjamin Lincoln House *(opposite)*

The home of Major General Benjamin Lincoln was built in Hingham in 1733. General Lincoln served in the Continental Army and was present for the British surrender of two major revolutionary battles at Yorktown, Virginia and Saratoga, New York. The home is a National Historic Landmark.

Old Ship Church *(above and opposite)*

Built in 1681 in the English Gothic style, the Old Ship Church in Hingham is one of the oldest houses of worship in North America that is still in use. The early Puritan builders may have been shipbuilders as well, since the oak beams of the church ceiling take on the appearance of an inverted ship's frame. Old Ship Church is a National Historic Landmark.

Lincoln Statue

A bronze statue of Abraham Lincoln faces the home of his ancestor, Samuel Lincoln, who emigrated from Hingham, England in 1637. Created by sculptor Charles Keck, the pensive President sits in an area known as the Lincoln Historic District. The sculpture's inscription reads: "Lincoln. With malice toward none. With charity for all."

Iron Horse

Brandishing a torch and sword, this mighty barefoot figure on horseback is a tribute to Hingham's men and women who served in the armed forces. His shield bares the inscription "Pro Patria et Gloria" (For Country and Glory). Looking out toward Hingham's inner harbor, the bronze war memorial, *Iron Horse,* was purchased in 1929.

Weir River Farm

Situated on a picturesque hillside, Weir
River Farm, a property of the Trustee of
Reservations, is one of Hingham's last working
farms. The grounds include a 1.5-mile hiking
path which accesses a large network of trails
in neighboring Wompatuck State Park and the
Triphammer Conservation Area. The farm also
offers educational programs and events.

Around the Barnyard *(top and bottom)*

What began as a visiting barnyard in 2000 has transformed into a 10-acre working farm that provides locally-grown produce, meat, and eggs. Historic Weir River Farm was donated to the Trustees of Reservations by renowned artist, Polly Thayer Starr. Visitors can join in and get their hands dirty at the working barnyard and 3.5-acre market garden.

World's End

Outdoor enthusiasts fully appreciate World's End in Hingham, with its 4.5 miles of tree-lined carriage paths designed by Frederick Law Olmstead. It is a naturalist's paradise whose woodlands and marshes are a habitat for hundreds of delicate native plants and birds.

Nature's Refuge

World's End in Hingham is a 251-acre landscape that features open hillsides, shady woodland paths, as well as sweeping views of the Boston skyline. The Trustees of Reservations prevented it from becoming a possible site for a nuclear power plant in 1967, and today it is enjoyed by hikers, horseback riders, and cross-country skiers.

Wooded Paradise

Just 15 miles from the city of Boston, World's End in Hingham provides a quiet natural refuge. Carriage trails, designed by Frederick Law Olmstead, were part of a development that was planned by wealthy businessman, John Brewer, during the late 1800s. The homes were never built, but the well-maintained carriage trails still remain.

Protected Retreat

Like tiny golden jewels, native plants bloom
and thrive at World's End Conservation
Area. The Trustees of Reservations acquired
World's End in Hingham and made it a
public park in 1967. The area was once
considered for the site of the United
Nations; fortunately, New York City was
chosen instead.

Hingham Yacht Club and Marina

The setting sun marks the end of another busy day at the Hingham Yacht Club and Marina. Established in 1895, the club hosts prestigious national championship races as well as a weekly local regatta. Its highly respected Junior Sailing Program has produced hundreds of capable sailors and racers.

Cozy Moorings

With the deep greenery of World's End Conservation Area as their backdrop, sun-drenched sailboats bob in Hingham Bay. The Hingham Yacht Club and Marina is located at the tip of Crow Point. Guest moorings are available on a first-come-first-serve basis.

South Shore Sunset

The spectacular view from the Hingham Yacht Club and Marina is painted with a fiery palette, framing the Boston skyline with red, gold, and orange. Commuters who live in quaint, suburban South Shore towns can travel to work via commuter boats provided by the Massachusetts Bay Transportation Authority (MBTA).

Best Seat in the House

The setting sun puts on quite a show for a lone kayaker at the end of the day in Hingham. Hingham Harbor is a prime cast-off spot for South Shore kayakers, being within reach of numerous points of interest such as Boston's Harbor Islands National Park, which include beautiful Button, Ragged, Sarah, and Langlee Islands.

Hingham Bathing Beach

Sun-drenched clam flats warm the shallow waters of Hingham Harbor, making for some unexpectedly comfortable swimming temperatures at Bathing Beach. This small beach, within walking distance from town, provides residents and visitors with exceptional views of the Harbor Islands as well as boats moored in the inner harbor.

Gulls in Flight

Seagulls soar above the crystal blue waters of Bathing Beach in Hingham. All along the South Shore's coastline, wildlife is abundant both above and below the water. Hingham was originally called "Bare Cove," perhaps because of the sprawling clam flats that are apparent at low tide.

Telegraph Hill

Atop a small peninsula in Hull Village, the Fort Revere outlook tower peeks out over the tree line of Telegraph Hill. Historic Fort Revere Park is an 8-acre historic site that includes an observation tower as well as a military history museum. From this vantage point, the military could keep watch over Boston Harbor and neighboring bays.

Fort Revere Park *(above)*

Overlooking Allerton, Fort Revere Park
includes the remains of two fortifications
from where the U.S. military kept watch of
Hingham, Quincy, and Dorchester Bays.
The park offers breathtaking vistas of Boston
Harbor and the Atlantic Ocean. Summer
events include military reenactments and
family movies under the stars.

Echos of the Past *(opposite)*

Exploring the fortifications at Fort Revere
Park, with their barred windows, fireplaces,
and tunnels, offers a glimpse of New
England's historic past. The park includes
a small military history museum where
exciting revolutionary stories come to life.

U.S. Lifesaving Station, Hull

Point Allerton U.S. Lifesaving Station, circa 1889, offers intriguing exhibits depicting a long tradition of selfless humanitarian efforts including the story of heroic station keeper, Joshua James. With the help of his valiant crews, he saved more than 1,000 lives over six decades of service. Also offered are lectures, workshops, and rowing programs.

Graves Lighthouse

Built in 1905 on a small island near Boston's North Channel, the 113-foot-high Graves Lighthouse remains an active navigational aid. Unpainted, the surf-swept tower is constructed of local granite. It was converted to solar power in 2001. The lighthouse's tiny island is part of the Boston Harbor Islands National Recreation Area.

Ebbing Tide

Boats await the incoming tide at Hull's Nantasket Beach. Whether boating, surfing, swimming, or just people watching, Nantasket Beach, with its shops, restaurants, and magnificent views, has been a popular summertime vacation retreat for Boston area families for decades.

Nantasket Beach Reservation

Nantasket Beach Reservation comprises
26 acres all along 1.3 miles of waterfront.
It is maintained by the Massachusetts
Department of Conservation and
Recreation. The late 1800s was the heyday
of Nantasket Beach, as it grew to become
a popular vacation destination, having the
largest summer hotel in the country.

Paragon Carousel *(top and bottom)*

Paragon Park offered the ultimate in family-style entertainment on Nantasket Beach. The iconic amusement park closed in 1984, however the park's clock tower and beautiful, hand-carved carousel still remain. The 1928 carousel is operational and is undergoing a historic renovation via the Friends of the Paragon Carousel.

Seaside Carnival *(opposite)*

A colorful carnival Ferris wheel at Nantasket Beach attests to the spirit of an amusement park of days gone by. Many Boston area families can recall warm summer nights enjoying the traditional rides at Paragon Park including the clickity-clack of the Giant Coaster, a wooden wonder built in 1917.

Rooms with a View *(top and bottom)*

The magnificent homes along Atlantic
Avenue in Cohasset enjoy spectacular ocean
views. Cohasset, from an Algonquian word
meaning "long rocky place," possesses the
natural beauty that draws visitors and film
makers alike. The 1987 film, *The Witches of
Eastwick*, was filmed here.

Quintessential New England

Nestled between Hull and Hingham, just 20 miles south of Boston, the town of Cohasset boasts a beautiful rocky coastline of charming harbors and outstanding ocean vistas. Cohasset incorporated in 1770 when it broke away from Hingham to become its own town.

Minot's Ledge Light

Boaters have the best view of Minot's Lighthouse, although there are also many great viewing points from the shore. The first lighthouse was a 70-foot structure that sat precariously atop iron pilings in 1849. In 1851, it succumbed to a great storm, taking the lives of two keepers: Joseph Wilson and Joseph Antoine.

The lighthouse was replaced in 1860, built solidly on the sunken ledge with over 3,000 tons of Quincy granite, and has withstood decades of heavy storms. Much to the relief of lightkeepers, the 114-foot tower was automated in 1947 and converted to solar power in 1983.

Minot Replica (*top*)

On Cohasset's Government Island is a replica of Minot's Lighthouse lantern room where visitors can learn to appreciate the size and strength of the nearby offshore structure. The lantern room houses an original Fresnel lens that was once used in the lighthouse.

Keepers' Memorial (*bottom*)

Joseph Antoine and Joseph Wilson were two young lightkeepers who lost their lives in the infamous 1851 "Minot's Light Storm." The pair were keepers of the original lighthouse, whose safety, being that it was built upon iron pilings, was often scrutinized by previous lightkeepers. This fitting memorial was dedicated in 2000 by local residents.

Cohasset Common *(top)*

Cohasset Town Hall, community center, three churches, and dozens of period homes including the Capt. Smith House (1857), the Capt. Tower House (1802), and the Josiah Bates House (1713), surround this quintessential New England green space. It's where locals meet for concerts, church services, and the Christmas tree lighting.

Cohasset Harbor *(bottom and opposite)*

South Shore boaters enjoy the pristine and peaceful setting of Cohasset Harbor. The marina is a cozy spot tucked away from nearby open waters. Within just a short walk, sailors can take full advantage of landlubber hospitalities including restaurants, cafés, and lodging.

Cohasset Yacht Club *(top, bottom, and opposite)*

Cohasset Yacht Club has been meeting the needs of this South Shore sailing community since 1894. Sailing lessons for adults and juniors, exciting regattas, fishing tournaments, and more are just some of the activities enjoyed by over 200 members and their families. Cohasset Yacht Club members include some of the most prestigious sailing champions in the country.

Life in a Small Town

The quaint, picture-perfect setting of
small- town Cohasset excercises all of the
senses. A pair of runners enjoy the winding,
flower-lined roads of this beautiful seaside
community, where each season unveils a
splendor all its own.

Mill Bridge

The pristine Gulf River flows beneath the Mill Bridge in Cohasset. This tidal estuary, between Scituate and Cohasset, has a delicate ecosystem that supports a wide variety of fish, plants, and wildlife. The Gulf Association is an organization working to protect the river through conservation efforts, education, and special events.

First Parish Church *(above)*

First Parish Church was founded in 1634 by Reverend John Lothrop, who settled in Scituate after being banished from England for leading a congregation in secret. His new congregation was made up of settlers from County Kent, England called the "Men of Kent." During the 19th century, the church was frequented by author Henry David Thoreau.

Stained-Glass Memento *(opposite)*

The beautiful stained-glass window of the First Parish Church depicts a 19th-century vessel that honors its seafaring parishioners. The previous church meeting house was destroyed by fire in 1879. Beyond repair, the bell forged by Paul Revere was melted down and sold as smaller bells to fund the new building that was dedicated in 1881.

Cudworth House and Barn *(top and bottom)*

The Cudworth House and Barn in Scituate reveal a glimpse into the life of some of the earliest South Shore residents. The existing house was built in 1797 around a chimney, which was all that remained of the previous structure after a fire. Today, it is a museum, complete with period artifacts and furnishings, and run by the Scituate Historical Society.

Lawson Tower *(opposite)*

In 1902, the wife of millionaire Thomas W. Lawson complained that a water tank was spoiling the views from their Scituate estate, "Dreamworld." Lawson hid the tank with a beautiful, 153-foot tower replicating a castle turret. Complete with chiming bells and sweeping ocean views. It was added to the National Register of Historic places in 1976.

Elephant Tales *(above and left)*

Prominent Boston businessman, Thomas W. Lawson, who made his home in Scituate, was enamored with elephants. Believing they brought good luck, he managed to accumulate a large collection of elephant figurines and momentos at his "Dreamworld" estate. The collection comprised approximately 3,000 jade, bronze, wood, and ivory elephants from all corners of the world.

Lawson donated land, now the town green, to the town of Scituate and paid for the beloved bronze elephant trio that has delighted residents and visitors since 1919.

Soldiers & Sailors Monument *(opposite)*

The Soldiers & Sailors Monument proudly honors Scituate's Civil War veterans. The bronze and granite monument, located in Lawson Common, was dedicated in 1918.

ERECTED BY THE
TOWN OF SCITUATE
IN MEMORY OF ITS
SOLDIERS AND SAILORS
1861 — 1865

A Victorian for the Arts *(opposite)*

The James Library and Center for the Arts in Norwell enlightens the South Shore with music, art, and literature. Built in 1874, the 19th-century Victorian is Norwell's oldest, and perhaps, busiest library, offering music lessons, concerts, puppet shows, art exhibits, seasonal story times, and historic literary events.

Union Mission Chapel *(above)*

This tiny church, nestled in the cool shade of towering New England pines, was built in 1885. The Union Mission Chapel is located on Old Oaken Bucket Road in Scituate.

Scituate Lighthouse (top)

To aid ships into Scituate's shallow harbor, a 25-foot stone tower was built in 1811 at Cedar Point and went into service in 1812. After decades of neglect, a restoration was initiated by the Daughters of the American Revolution in 1907, and it has since undergone periodic updates. Today, the now 50-foot tower is the country's eleventh oldest lighthouse.

Scituate Town Pier (bottom)

Since its incorporation in 1636, Scituate has maintained a long maritime heritage. Within one of the most picturesque harbors on the South Shore, Scituate Harbor Marina shelters a large number of recreational boats. Great restaurants, shopping, and historic sites are all within walking distance.

Chilly Namesake

Boaters return from a recreational fishing
excursion on a calm afternoon, perhaps
in search of striped bass, cod, or tuna. The
name "Scituate" is derived from the Native
American word "Satuit," which means "cold
brook." Its coastline varies from flat, sandy
salt marshes to rugged granite bedrock.

North River

Meandering through South Shore marshes and spilling out into the Atlantic Ocean, the North River separates the coastal towns of Scituate and Marshfield. The North River Wildlife Sanctuary in Marshfield features a boardwalk, where you can enjoy a half-mile stroll through cattail marshes and discover an array of South Shore birds and wildlife.

Working on the River

A boater prepares for a day of exploration along the North River. This pristine tidal river is an 8-mile stretch that is mostly salt water fed by freshwater streams. At high tide, fish such as trout and bass abound, while shellfish beds along the river are ideal for clamming at low tide.

Green Harbor Beach

Cottages line inviting Green Harbor Beach in Marshfield. During the 1860s, the area was frequented by famous American artist, Winslow Homer, who had resident relatives. It is believed that the impressionist master was inspired by Marshfield beaches and used them in both his oil and watercolor paintings.

Barefoot Days of Summer

Beachgoers leave their cares, and their flip-flops, behind to enjoy a summertime frolic along Marshfield's Green Harbor Beach. It is one of Marshfield's most kid-friendly beaches, offering crystal clear, calm waters. The Green Harbor Beach Association hosts events such as a July 4th sandcastle contest and movies on the beach.

Rexhame Beach

Rexhame Beach is a favorite South Shore hangout for tourists and locals on any busy summer day. The beach is separated from the mainland by salt marshes, and the dunes protect the mainland from fierce winter storms. Dune preservation is provided by the Marshfield Beach Restoration and Preservation Association.

Brant Rock Beach

Huge boulders, toppled one upon another, provide secret places for small sea life that thrive in hidden tidal pools. Marshfield's Brant Rock Beach offers both rocky and sandy areas. Tourists find that the nearby ice cream shop completes the perfect summer outing. Don't forget to include Fido—Brant Rock Beach is a dog-friendly zone.

Humarock Beach *(above and pages 86–87)*

A catamaran has a perfect place to launch at Humarock Beach. "Humarock" is derived from the Wampanoag word meaning "seashell place." Humarock is a long peninsula separated from the mainland for the most part by the South River and accessible by bridge from Marshfield or by boat from Scituate.

Humble Law Office *(top)*

Located on the grounds of the Winslow House, this humble building served as the law office of Daniel Webster. Webster was known as the "Defender of the Constitution." He tried and won over 150 cases before the Supreme Court. Many dignitaries visited this small space that also served as Webster's horticultural library.

Farmer of Marshfield *(bottom)*

Daniel Webster Estate and Heritage Center includes Webster's home as well as other buildings used for breeding cattle and cultivating the soil. Webster was not only a Massachusetts Senator, he also served as Secretary of State for Presidents William Henry Harrison, John Tyler, and Millard Fillmore. Webster died in 1852.

Daniel Webster Estate

Daniel Webster, famous lawyer and Senator of Massachusetts, purchased the home and farmland of Captain John Thomas in 1832. Known as the "Farmer of Marshfield," Webster cultivated the land and planted trees obtained from various places throughout the world. Many of these trees still grace the estate grounds.

Isaac Winslow House

Occupied by generations of Winslows, including those who founded the town of Marshfield, the Winslow House was built circa 1699 by Judge Isaac Winslow, the grandson of a *Mayflower* Pilgrim. It was since owned by many local dignitaries, including Senator Daniel Webster. The home is listed on the National Register of Historic Places.

Historic Herb Garden

The grounds of the historic Isaac Winslow House are graced with a fragrant period herb garden. The home features period furnishings, artifacts, and historic documents, and is open to the public from mid-May to Columbus Day. The Tea Room is also available for functions.

King Caesar House

This 1809 Federal-style mansion was home
to a legendary Duxbury shipping family.
Ezra Weston II (1772–1842) lived here with
his wife, Jerusha. Dubbed "King Caesar"
for his success, his shipping firm was the
largest commercial trading company on the
South Shore. Today, the Duxbury Rural and
Historical Society operates the museum.

Ezra Weston House Gardens *(above cnd right)*

During spring and summer, the grounds of the stately home of Ezra Weston II, the "King Caesar House," turn lush and colorful with the beautiful flower garden maintained by the Community Garden Club of Duxbury. The grounds also include a formal herb garden that is lovingly cared for by the Duxbury Garden Club.

Nathaniel Winsor, Jr. House *(above)*

This historic Federal-style home was built
in 1807 for Nathaniel Winsor, Jr., the son
of a wealthy shipbuilding and shipping
mogul. Winsor inherited his father's business
and went on to build a fleet of vessels that
participated in worldwide trade. The famous
home now houses the Duxbury Rural &
Historical Society.

An Extraordinary Mansion *(opposite)*

The beautifully landscaped grounds of
the Nathaniel Winsor, Jr. House include a
brick patio, pergola, and charming statuary.
The breathtaking views of Duxbury Bay
make this a desirable location for wedding
receptions and other special events.

Seth Sprague House

Duxbury's Old Shipbuilding Historic District features stately homes built from fortunes accumulated during the 19th-century shipping and shipbuilding industries that escalated shortly after the American Revolution. Following in his father's footsteps in businesses that supplied local shipyards, Seth Sprague, Jr. built this home in 1813.

Gershom Bradford House

Gershom Bradford was a Duxbury sea captain who commanded nearly a dozen vessels. His descendants, the last of four generations to occupy the Gershom Bradford House, bequeathed it to the Duxbury Rural & Historical Society in 1968. The historic home still has all its original period furnishings and decor.

Early American Barn *(above and left)*

Part of the John Alden House Museum, this replica of the Alden's original barn that was built circa 17th century, was built by Alden Kindred of America, Inc. Its design blends in with the original house, however it has been modernized to accommodate the many programs and events hosted throughout the year.

John Alden House Museum

The original Alden House was built in 1653 and has never been owned by any other family. Arriving on the *Mayflower* in 1620, John Alden and Priscilla Mullins were married around 1622. The story is told how John had set out as a messenger to ask Pricilla's hand in marriage for his friend Myles Standish, to which she is said to have replied, "Why do you not speak for yourself, John?" Their courtship commenced shortly after. The home and museum is overseen by the Alden Kindred of America, Inc., a group dedicated to preserving the history of the early Pilgrims. The organization's brick project allows donors to dedicate a brick in the Alden House walkway.

Bluefish River *(above and left)*

The Bluefish River lazily meanders through the historic town of Duxbury. During the late 18th and early 19th centuries, at the river's mouth, a thriving maritime trade industry dominated. Wharves were busy with shipments of charcoal, iron, lumber, as well as fish. Today, it is a peaceful and incredibly beautiful suburb.

Summer Along the Bluefish River *(opposite)*

At the mouth of the Bluefish River in Duxbury is the Old Shipbuilding Historic District. Many beautiful 19th-century homes along the riverfront once belonged to sea captains and shipping magnates. Here, a sprawling backyard greets crystal blue waters making for an inviting summertime setting.

The Bug

Marking the dangerous shoal off Saquish
Head, Duxbury Pier Light, built in 1871,
has withstood years of brutal New England
storms. The squat light, known as "Bug Light"
or "The Bug" by locals, has three stories
that include living space and a watchroom.
Automated in 1964, Duxbury residents have
contributed to its preservation.

Duxbury Pier (top)

Recreational sculling boats sit in the midday sun on Duxbury Pier. Duxbury Bay is dotted with recreational craft of all kinds. The ideal location and seemingly unspoiled surroundings make it a desirable port for boaters.

Sung Harbor (bottom)

Duxbury Pier, in Snug Harbor, is a picturesque boating venue. The basin offers amazing views of the bay and Duxbury Bay Maritime School. Incorporated in 1997, the maritime school offers sailing, rowing, and kayaking programs, as well as races. The campus includes Clifford Hall, a popular venue available for special events.

South Shore Sunrise

A typical Duxbury morning begins with a
spectacular sunrise. Pilgrim Myles Standish
named the town after a wooded area in his
hometown in Great Britain. The town was
founded in 1637 and has become one of
Boston's most affluent suburbs.

Awash in Color

Pinks and purples are reflected in Duxbury's shallow harbor in the early morning hours. With so many brooks, rivers, bogs, and marshes, nearly half of the town's area is water, adding much to the character of the region. It is one of the area's largest cranberry producers and is well known for its oyster beds and clam flats.

Major John Bradford House *(top and opposite)*

Descendant of Governor William Bradford who arrived on the *Mayflower*, Major John Bradford was commander of Plymouth military forces and helped to incorporate the town of Plymouth. The Kingston home was built in 1714 and is listed in the National Register of Historic Places. Today, it is home to the Jones River Village Historical Society.

Mary's Garden *(bottom)*

The Bradford Homestead includes a threshing barn and period garden. The historic garden—Mary's Garden—was named in 1997 for well-known Kingston resident, Mary Rushton, a longtime member of the Jones River Village Historical Society.

Jenny Grist Mill (*above*)

Early Pilgrims learned the art of grinding corn from Native Americans. The grist mill made the task of mortar and pestle obsolete with a faster and more efficient way to provide for the growing community. Jenny Grist Mill and Museum in Plymouth has exhibits, living history tours, and educational programs.

17th-Century Innovation (*opposite*)

John Jenny introduced the power of water to Plymouth by building the country's first grist mill in 1636, greatly contributing to the industrial growth in the community. A replica of Jenny's mill was built on the same location along Town Brook that runs through the town and flows into Plymouth Harbor.

Brewster Gardens *(top and bottom)*

William Brewster first tended the original garden plot in Plymouth in 1620. Pilgrims first settled here because of the abundance of fresh water from the many brooks and streams in the area. Not far from Plymouth Rock, Brewster Gardens is a waterfront park that comprises this first historic plot as well as a pleasant nature trail.

Plymouth's Town Brook

From mid-April to mid-May, schools of
herring migrate from the Atlantic Ocean and
head upstream via Town Brook in search
of fresh water ponds in which to spawn.
Herring were used by the early Pilgrims
and Native Americans as a natural fertilizer.
Today, visitors flock to Jenny Grist Mill in
spring to view the upstream migration.

1749
COURT HOUSE
MUSEUM

FREE ADMISSION

Court House Museum (*opposite*)

Built in 1749, Plymouth's historic Court House is the oldest wooden courthouse in the country. Listed in the National Register of Historic Places, it opened as a museum in 1970 and houses many of Plymouth's historic artifacts and documents. Located in the center of town, the museum also houses an 1828 fire engine and town hearse.

Hedge House (*top*)

Hedge House was built in 1809 by Captain William Hammatt, and was purchased in 1830 by Thomas Hedge, a successful merchant. The Federal-style home was occupied by Hedge families until 1918. Today, the home is owned by the Plymouth Antiquarian Society, who arranged to move the home to its present waterfront location.

Plymouth's Historic District (*bottom*)

Plymouth's downtown-harbor area includes many historically significant structures. Plymouth Historic District Commission recognizes the need to preserve these buildings whose architectural designs span three centuries. The Commission provides renovation and alteration guidelines that protect their architectural heritage.

Historic Architecture *(above and left)*

Plymouth's Historic District includes many fine examples of period architecture. Above, the Plymouth Memorial Building has been beautifully renovated and serves as a unique entertainment venue featuring concerts, trade shows, and family entertainment.

Myles Standish Monument *(opposite)*

English military officer, Myles Standish, one of the area's first settlers, was heavily involved in the development of Plymouth Colony. Captain Standish is memorialized with a 116-foot granite tower, built in 1898, in Myles Standish Monument State Reservation. The tower's 125-step climb culminates in sweeping panoramic views of Plymouth Harbor and the Blue Hills.

Forefathers Monument *(above)*

Plymouth's *National Monument to the Fore-fathers* features figures that depict the virtues of the Pilgrims. Designed in 1888 by Boston sculptor, Hammatt Billings, the inscription reads: "National Monument to the Forefathers. Erected by a grateful people in remembrance of their labors, sacrifices and sufferings for the cause of civil and religious liberty."

Pilgrim Hall *(opposite)*

Pilgrim Hall Museum preserves the heritage of the country's earliest settlers, from their brave journey in 1620, to the courageous first years of building homes and communities in the New World. The museum has an amazing collection of Pilgrim artifacts including the sword of Capt. Myles Standish, the bible of William Bradford, and the cradle of the colony's first-born, Peregrine White.

Landing Place of the Pilgrims

Although there is no official account of the Pilgrims actually stepping onto a rock during their 1620 landing, this seaside monument houses a rock that marks the traditional site where William Bradford and the Pilgrims disembarked from the *Mayflower* and founded Plymouth Colony.

Friend to the First Settlers

Designed by Cyrus Dallin, this bronze statue of Massasoit was dedicated by the Improved Order of Red Men in 1921. Massasoit was a leader of the Wampanoag—a Native American tribe who lived in areas now known as Massachusetts and Rhode Island. In 1621 the Wampanoag and Pilgrims celebrated harvest together.

Life Aboard the *Mayflower II* *(above and left)*

The first Pilgrims epitomized bravery on an enormous scale, having to spend more than ten weeks at sea under the most dangerous circumstances. Aboard the *Mayflower II* are many necessities, such as tools and utensils, used during their precarious voyage.

Mayflower II *(opposite)*

Imagine crossing the Atlantic on a vessel 106-feet long and just 25-feet wide. The full-scale reproduction of the *Mayflower* made that voyage in 1957 and can be boarded at Plimoth Plantation. The *Mayflower II* was built in Devon, England and is complete with carefully re-created details that help conceptualize what life was like living aboard a 17th-century ship.

Wampanoag Cuisine

The Wampanoag Homesite at Plimoth Plantation is a living exhibit that depicts the 17th-century lives of the Wampanoag tribe. Using only ingredients that were available during the 1600s, meals, including delicious New England seafood, are prepared over open fires and served in hand-carved bowls.

Wampanoag Culture *(left)*

Plimoth Plantation's Wampanoag Homesite is located along the Eel River. All Homesite staff are Native people and have re-created the traditional lives of their ancestors. They make baskets, build houses, and tend crops of tobacco and corn. Here, a Native uses fire to hollow out a tree in the first steps of canoe making.

Coastal Heritage *(right)*

A Wampanoag woman is busy cooking. At the Wampanoag Homesite, staff dress in accurate traditional clothing and perform day-to-day tasks and chores typical to 17th-century life on coastal New England.

Tending the Garden

The 17th-Century English Village at Plimoth Plantation is where history comes to life. Colonial role players re-create Pilgrim work and play in the Museum's reconstruction of fortified Plymouth as it might have looked in 1627. They tend gardens, build houses, care for rare breeds of livestock, and more.

English Village

Colonial role players emerge from timber-framed, thatch-roofed homes and go about their chores as the original residents would have done in the 17th century. This living historic exhibit is an eye-opening experience depicting both the hope and the harsh realities of early Pilgrim life.

Gurnet Lighthouse

Plymouth (Gurnet) Light was first built in
1803 as two separate wooden structures that
were spaced thirty feet apart. America's first
twin lighthouses became a lone beacon when
the northeast tower was torn down in 1924.
The Gurnet is the oldest freestanding wooden
lighthouse in the country and also known to
have the first woman lightkeeper.

Plymouth Breakwater *(top)*

Before Plymouth breakwater was built, many ships were wrecked from dangerous storms that came out of the southwest. Some 4 million tons of limestone and rock were used to build the 1,710-yard barrier that protects Plymouth Sound.

White Horse Beach *(bottom)*

The South Shore offers many stretches of beautiful white-sand beaches. White Horse Beach is located in Manomet, a village of Plymouth. It is the traditional spot for Independence Day bon fires and fireworks that are wildly anticipated each July 3rd.

Ralph Granata is a portrait, editorial, and commercial photographer serving the Boston metropolitan area. His work has been published in books, local publications, and news outlets. In addition, his work has been shown in galleries in the Boston area. Ralph is passionate about creating images that convey a message or tell a story. He lives in Quincy, Massachusetts with his wife, Cindy and their dog Baxter. To learn more about Ralph visit his website at www.ralphgranata.com.

Born and raised in Gloucester, Massachusetts, writer and award-winning graphic designer, Sara Day, continues to be inspired by the beauty of New England. A long career working with publishers, photographers, and advertising agencies, Sara uses her talents to create exquisite photo journals as well as promotional materials. She also enjoys capturing the majesty of this unique place in her oil paintings. Visit www.sypdesign.com and www.twinlightspub.com to see more of her work.